Original title:
Sometimes Life Is Just Tacos

Author: Natalia Harrington
ISBN HARDBACK: 978-1-80566-130-6
ISBN PAPERBACK: 978-1-80566-425-3

Melodies of the Street Food

On corners where the laughter flows,
Food trucks gather like friendly crows.
Each sizzle and pop whispers delight,
Calling us in for a savory bite.

With toppings piled high, a playful stack,
Every crunch adds joy, no missing knack.
Saucy dreams wrapped in soft embrace,
Who knew a meal could win such a race?

Filling the Void with Each Bite

A hungry heart seeks warmth and cheer,
A tortilla wraps up every fear.
With guacamole, a soft green hug,
Each bite a dance, a merry tug.

Laughter spills like juice from lime,
In between bites, we find our rhyme.
Sharing tales, we savor the craze,
Chasing flavors in a hungry daze.

Bits of Spice and Serendipity

A dash of chili, a sprinkle of fun,
These little moments keep us on the run.
From cart to mouth, our cravings pursue,
Unexpected delights, just waiting for you.

With salsa that dances, so bright on the tongue,
Every encounter feels eternally young.
Bits of cilantro to elevate the day,
In every bite, a little ballet.

The Delicious Path of Discovery

We wander the streets with our hearts in tow,
In search of treasures, our appetites grow.
A taco's a map to flavors unknown,
With every new find, a wisdom we've grown.

The crunch of the shell, the melt of the cheese,
Who knew exploration could come with such ease?
With each tasty turn, we share a big grin,
For life's little moments make the best of kin.

The Texture of Togetherness

In a shell so crisp and bright,
We gather close, a fond delight.
Chopped onions dance and sway,
As laughter joins the fray.

With every bite, a crunching sound,
A tasty bond that knows no bounds.
Salsa splashes, colors ignite,
A fiesta feels so right.

A Journey of Taste

The toppings line up for their cue,
Avocado green, and cheese so blue.
Each flavor leads a joyful race,
On a plate, a tasty space.

Tomato chunks like little suns,
Spicy bites that tickle and run.
We're on a ride, a flavor train,
In each wrap, fun we gain.

Night of the Nachos

Under stars, the nachos glow,
Cheesy streams begin to flow.
With jalapeños stacked up high,
We crunch and munch while voices fly.

Every chip a party guest,
In this bowl, we feel so blessed.
A mountain made of blissful treats,
Crunching laughter, heartful beats.

The Joy of Each Bite

Beneath the moon, we take our seats,
With taco stacks, our love repeats.
Each spicy taste brings joy anew,
Every bite feels like a view.

We toast with guac, a creamy cheer,
In our hearts, the flavor's clear.
In this moment, simple and bright,
Every taco feels just right.

Taste Buds and Heartstrings

Crunchy shell, a tasty hug,
Wrapped in dreams, oh what a drug.
Salsa dances, hot and bold,
Each bite a laugh, a joy to hold.

Cheese cascades like falling stars,
With every layer, it raises bars.
A sprinkle of love, a dash of spice,
This feast of fun is oh so nice.

Where Flavor Meets Fate

In a world where toppings reign,
Each choice a chance, a flavorful gain.
Beans and guac in a fierce embrace,
A taco twist, the perfect chase.

Lettuce whispers a crunchy tune,
Potatoes waltz beneath the moon.
Where sauce meets cheese, oh what a bliss,
A culinary hug, you can't miss.

Life's Savory Surprises

A taco truck rumbles down the street,
With every stop, a tasty treat.
Surprises hide in every fold,
A story of flavors yet untold.

Jalapeños bring a fiery cheer,
With laughter shared, we've nothing to fear.
Avocado smiles, looking so cool,
Life's spicy punch, never a dull school.

Unraveled in a Tortilla

With layers piled, the world stands still,
A tender wrap, it's food, it's thrill.
Laughter spills like salsa's pour,
In every bite, there's always more.

Each fold reveals a savory quest,
In the kitchen, we're all truly blessed.
Unraveled joy, both wrapped and free,
A taco life is pure glee.

Spice Up the Ordinary

In a world of bread and butter,
Let's add a twist to make it better.
With salsa and guac, let's create a scene,
Where every bite's a taste machine.

Forget the bland and dull routine,
Add some zest, make it a cuisine.
A sprinkle of laughter, a dash of cheer,
In each crunchy bite, joy's always near.

Wrapped in Delight

Beneath the moon, so soft and bright,
I unwrap my dinner, pure delight.
With layers of love that just can't fail,
Every mouthful tells a tasty tale.

Folded with care, so snug and warm,
Like life's great moments, it's the norm.
From tacos to laughs, it's magic, you see,
In every wrap, there's a smile for me.

Meandering Through Tasty Adventures

Let's journey far to taco land,
Where every flavor is close at hand.
With a dash of joy wrapped up in each bite,
Life's a taco party, shining bright!

Chasing dreams with hot sauce flair,
Savoring moments we willingly share.
From spicy to sweet, take a chance today,
In this taco quest, we're here to play!

A Cornucopia of Joy

A colorful plate, a joyful spread,
With hints of humor where dreams are bred.
Laughter's the seasoning, love's the main dish,
In every taco, there lies a wish.

Corn, beans, and giggles piled high,
With creamy avocados, who needs to fly?
A feast for the senses, each bite a surprise,
In this joyful journey, we'll claim the prize!

The Comfort of Crunch

When joy is wrapped in crispy shells,
I take a bite and all's well.
Toppings dance like confetti bright,
Every flavor feels just right.

Salsa spills like laughter shared,
With every crunch, no one is scared.
Cheese cascades in cheesy dreams,
Life's better with taco-themed schemes.

Layered Joys on a Plate

With layers stacked like a perfect day,
Beans and beef in a warm display.
Guacamole joins the endless fun,
A fiesta bursting, never done.

In every bite, a tale unfolds,
Of spicy journeys and flavors bold.
Sour cream smiles on top so bright,
Each taste a giggle, pure delight.

Soft Shell Serenade

Wrapped in warmth like a hug that's tight,
Soft shells sing in the pale moonlight.
A gentle crunch, a playful tease,
With every bite, my heart's at ease.

Spicy salsa twirls with glee,
It's a party, just for me!
Tomatoes dance, cilantro sways,
In taco dreams, I'll spend my days.

A Fiesta of Flavor

In a world where the tortillas sing,
Life's a fiesta, let joy take wing.
Chilies and cheese create a show,
Each flavor's story begins to flow.

Crispy bits, and layers divine,
With every bite, all's just fine.
So gather 'round, let's laugh and cheer,
For taco love is always near.

Tasting Moments of Euphoria

A tortilla wraps a little joy,
Filled with cheese, oh what a toy!
Lettuce dances with a crunch so fine,
In every bite, laughter's intertwine.

Guacamole dreams on a sunny plate,
Tomatoes smile, oh what a fate!
With every munch, the world's aglow,
In this tasty treat, we steal the show.

Curb Your Hunger

The sun shines down on a spicy feast,
A bit of lime, to say the least.
If hunger strikes with a wild groove,
A taco's dance gets you in the mood.

Chili's heat plays a lively tune,
As we gobble up under the moon.
Funny faces, bites so bold,
Each taco story, waiting to be told.

When Life Hands You Salsa

A scoop of salsa, a little dance,
With every dip, we take a chance.
Life's a party with chips in tow,
In each zesty bite, we laugh and glow.

A sprinkle of spice, oh what a thrill,
We face the day with a taco fill.
Facing challenges with zest and flair,
In the salsa swirl, we lighten care.

A Flavorful Mosaic

Colors collide in a tasty wrap,
Chiming flavors, a joyous clap.
Avocado whispers secrets sweet,
Each bite a journey, oh how neat!

Corn and beans in a snug embrace,
Funny faces as we pick up pace.
A mosaic of bites, laughter's tune,
We feast on joy, 'neath the silver moon.

Flavor Full Throttle

In a world that's cheesy and bright,
Crispy shells crunch with delight.
A fiesta of flavors, oh so bold,
Tales of guacamole joy unfold.

Salsa dances on chips with glee,
Limes twist as they sip on tea.
Beans and cheese in a merry twirl,
Who knew dinner could give a whirl?

Carnitas sing a savory song,
With every bite, you can't go wrong.
Variety piled in a tasty stack,
With a side of laughter, there's no lack.

In this kitchen, we laugh and play,
With every taco, we brighten the day.
Bring your appetite, don't be shy,
Together we'll munch until we fly!

Salsa and Stories Amid the Stars

up above, the stars gleam bright,
While tacos twinkle with pure delight.
Salsa spills like tales anew,
As friends gather 'round for a tasty view.

Each bite's a journey, flavors unwind,
Like stars in the night, each one's aligned.
Crunchy and tender, a perfect blend,
With every taco, laughter will send.

A mix of stories, a splash of fun,
Hands are messy, but we've just begun.
Add a sprinkle of spice, let it flow,
Together we share, let our joy grow.

Under the moonlight, our worries fade,
Coz tacos and tales never invade.
In this feast of friendship, we're never far,
Salsa and stories amid the stars.

Stacked High with Hope

On a plate where dreams are piled,
It's a tower of joy, always wild.
A mountain of salsa, a scoop of cheese,
With every bite, your heart can ease.

Tortillas wrap each little wish,
In this flavor fest, you'll find your bliss.
Roasted veggies, a colorful boom,
Come and savor the tasty zoom.

Layer upon layer, it's a stack of cheer,
With friends by your side, all worries clear.
Bite into laughter, let worries drop,
In this crunchy haven, we never stop.

Hope is seasoned, each taco glows,
With every filling, love only grows.
A delightful journey, served hot and bright,
Stacked high with joy, oh what a sight!

When Simplicity Meets Savory

In a world where flavors collide,
Simple pleasures, we won't hide.
A taco truck rolls with a wink,
Filling our hearts before we blink.

When freshness hits, you know it's true,
The taste of life in each savory cue.
Sour cream clouds and spices divine,
Every bite whispers, 'You're doing fine!'

Gather 'round, let's all unwind,
In tortilla wraps, joy we find.
Bite after bite, laughter in air,
In this taco dream, we have no care.

So here's to sharing, a flavorful ride,
Where joy is served up, and smiles abide.
In every simple, spicy embrace,
Life is a taco, a bright, warm place!

Moments Served with Guacamole

In a world of cheese and spice,
We roll our joys, we roll them nice.
Salsa drips, a smiling face,
Grab a chip, it's time to embrace.

Lettuce greedily stacked so high,
Beans for brains, oh me, oh my!
A squeeze of lime, the laughs ignite,
In this feast, all feels just right.

The Flavor of Everyday Bliss

Crispy shells, a crunchy cheer,
Each bite brings smiles, far and near.
A side of joy, a pinch of zest,
Who knew tacos could be the best?

With every layer, stories unfold,
Of dreams and giggles, joyful and bold.
Chili flakes with laughter mix,
Each meal dances, a tasty fix.

Tortilla Tales of Togetherness

Gather 'round, it's taco night,
Sharing is key, and oh, what a sight!
Toppings piled, like a mountain view,
Each bite a hug, warm and true.

Sour cream swirls, a creamy delight,
Friends around, hearts feeling light.
In every fold, our moments shine,
With every taco, our spirits entwine.

Embracing the Heat

Spicy salsa makes us laugh,
With every bite, we dance and chaff.
Hot sauce splatters like a joy parade,
In this fiesta, worries fade.

Life's a taco, never plain,
We toss in humor, we add the gain.
So bring the peppers, ignite the fun,
With every crunch, we've surely won.

The Dance of the Taco

In a shell so crisp and bright,
Filling wiggles, what a sight!
Sauce flows like a funky beat,
Join the party, bring your heat!

Lettuce sways, guac takes a bow,
Cilantro twirls, oh me, oh wow!
With every bite, the flavors sing,
What joy a taco can bring!

Moments Savored in Bites

Gather 'round, it's feast time,
Toppings stacked, oh so sublime!
Cheese cascades like a waterfall,
With each bite, we have a ball!

Salsa drips, a zesty tease,
A burst of joy like summer breeze.
Laughter flows, the plates do clatter,
In this moment, nothing's better!

Journey Through the Salsa Storm

Beware the spice, it's not for meek,
Each chip braves the salsa peak.
Dancing flavors whirl and spin,
In this fiesta, let's dig in!

Twists and turns in every crunch,
What a wild time for lunch!
Scoop and dip, don't miss a beat,
Here's a treat you can't defeat!

A Crunchy Revelation

The taco shell, it holds a dream,
A symphony of taste and cream.
In every layer, a surprise,
Take a bite and realize!

Jalapeños jump, beans take a ride,
All aboard, let's enjoy the tide!
A moment wrapped so tight and neat,
With every crunch, life's a treat!

Whimsical Wraps of Happiness

In a world made of tortillas, so soft and round,
Laughter spills out like salsa, delightful sound.
Wrap up your troubles, take a big bite,
Joy comes drizzled, everything feels just right.

Chasing pure bliss with every crunchy shell,
Sprinkled with stories that we love to tell.
A dash of the silly, a pinch of the fun,
With each tasty layer, we all come undone.

Flavorful Memories on Repeat

Life's a blend of spices, a good bit of zest,
Each moment, like guac, put to the test.
Mouthfuls of laughter, bites filled with cheer,
Remember the flavor, keep them all near.

When chips and salsa dance in the air,
We savor the good times, without a care.
Wrap those bright memories, let laughter unfold,
In each tasty moment, life's treasures are told.

Savoring Sunshine in Every Layer

Beneath all the layers, there's sunshine and fun,
Scoop up the giggles, let worries be done.
Lettuce and laughter, a colorful mix,
Taste all the joy, it's a savory fix.

Corn salsa smiles, a fiesta on a plate,
Each bite a reminder, let's celebrate fate.
So wrap up the magic, put on your best cheer,
With each delightful layer, happiness is near.

The Secret Ingredient Is You

What makes it special? Here's the big clue,
The crunch and the flavor, they come from you.
Add a sprinkle of kindness, a dash of delight,
In the taco of life, you're the heart, shining bright.

Laughter's the salsa, and joy's the fish,
Mix them together, oh what a wish!
Wrap it all up in your favorite style,
The secret to living? Just do it with a smile.

Patterns of Passion

In a world of lettuce and cheese,
We find joy with every single squeeze.
Salsa dancing on a warm shell,
Flavorful tales we know so well.

Onions chopped with laughter and glee,
A sprinkle of spice sets the heart free.
Jalapeños teasing with fiery heat,
In this culinary dance, we feel complete.

Tortilla dreams that spin and twirl,
Wrapped in stories that make us whirl.
Together we feast, no need for a map,
Just love on our plates, in this joyful trap.

Chasing beats of laughter in the night,
Under the stars, everything feels right.
With each bite, we celebrate this craze,
In flavors and friendships, we set ablaze.

Finding Harmony in Ingredients

Beneath the moon, the counter aglow,
Ingredients come together, a lively show.
Tomatoes blush in a vibrant dance,
Joining hands in a savory romance.

Cabbage crunches in pure delight,
Carried away in this playful light.
Together they form a perfect embrace,
Creating a feast, a scrumptious space.

Guacamole jerseys and chips that cheer,
A team united, no room for fear.
With each creation, our hearts collide,
In this kitchen symphony, we take pride.

As the utensils hum a merry tune,
The pockets fill up, we'll dance till noon.
Finding joy in every little bite,
With flavors like laughter, everything's bright.

The Happiness Cart

Rolling through town with a smile so wide,
A cart full of goodness, we take a ride.
Dancing with flavors, from sweet to bold,
Each tasty journey is waiting to unfold.

Churros and chips, everything's fine,
Hot sauce drips in a glorious line.
Sizzling meats wrapped up tight,
Our belly's the compass, leading us right.

Gather your friends, it's time to feast,
On soft-shell wonders, laughter increased.
With every crunch, our spirits soar,
This happiness cart is our open door.

Spices and giggles, hugs all around,
In this delicious moment, joy is found.
So come join the fun, let your heart sway,
In this cart of happiness, we play and play.

Tales of Corn and Love

From kernels of sweetness, romance grows,
In fields of flavors, love overflows.
Soft tortillas whisper soft dreams in the night,
Each bite a promise, everything feels right.

With a side of laughter, we gather near,
Stories unfold with every cheer.
Corn salsa sings of days gone by,
In each juicy bite, memories fly.

The grill's warm embrace, a fragrant delight,
Sharing these moments brings pure light.
Let's toast our tacos, with joy they bring,
In this feast of love, our hearts take wing.

So let's savor each moment, let's clink our cups,
In the tales of corn, our happiness erupts.
For in every tortilla, every twist and bend,
Are stories of laughter and love without end.

A Palette of Possibility

In a world full of spices, we twirl,
Chasing after laughter, a dancer's whirl.
With colors that burst, so vibrant, so bold,
Each bite a story, waiting to be told.

A dash of humor, a sprinkle of zest,
In this savory life, we feast and we jest.
Tortillas embracing, with fillings galore,
Together we savor, always wanting more.

The salsa's a wink, the guac's a tease,
Life's wild ride is like a taco breeze.
Wrapped tight in laughter, we share our delight,
In this joyful journey, every flavor feels right.

So gather your friends, let's make a parade,
In the kitchen of fun, our worries will fade.
With each crunchy bite, we giggle and cheer,
Life's recipe bubbles, bringing us near.

Chasing Flavorful Dreams

A taco truck rolls in, with dreams on the side,
Chasing flavors like rainbows, a culinary ride.
Each topping a whisper, a wish on the tongue,
A fiesta of wishes, forever young.

Lettuce so crisp, it dances on plates,
While cheese brings the comfort, and laughter awaits.
Salsa so spicy, it tickles our days,
In this silly dance, we all find new ways.

Tales of adventures, wrapped snug in a shell,
Life's spicy moments, we laugh and we yell.
With every taco crafted, a journey unfolds,
In flavors of joy, our story is told.

So let's chase these dreams with a twist and a taste,
Life is a banquet, let's not let it waste.
With every bite taken, we savor the scene,
In the kitchen of laughter, we reign as the queen.

Layers of Life

In this layered journey, we stack with a grin,
A tortilla of joy, where moments begin.
With salsa spilling tales, so tangy and bright,
Each flavor a layer, delighting the night.

A scoop of guacamole, smooth and so creamy,
Reminds us of laughter, oh so dreamy.
Onions bring laughter, while cilantro's a twist,
In life's perfect recipe, none can be missed.

With every creation, we build and we play,
Folding in memories that brighten the day.
An assembly of stories all wrapped in a fold,
Each bite a reminder, as life unfolds.

So let's share a taco and toast to the ride,
With layers of joy that we carry inside.
The crunch of adventure, the heat of the fun,
In this banquet of friendship, we've already won.

The Whirlwind of Ingredients

In a whirlwind of colors, we spiral with glee,
Chopping and mixing, just you and me.
The cilantro twirls round, with a spicy bouquet,
In this culinary dance, who needs ballet?

Tomatoes are giggling, the onions they cry,
As we throw in some cheese, reaching for the sky.
With laughter and ketchup, we create a storm,
In this tasty chaos, we find our own form.

With each sizzling moment, the kitchen delights,
A joyous explosion on taco-filled nights.
Burritos and nachos join in the fun,
Life's comical whirl, where we're all number one.

So grab your fiesta and swing to the beat,
In the complex dance of this savory treat.
With every bite taken, we echo in rhyme,
In this whirlwind of flavors, we're lost, oh sublime.

The Journey Through Spice Routes

On a quest for tasty treats,
I wander through vibrant streets.
Salsa dances, flavors cheer,
In this adventure, joy is near.

With each bite, a world unfolds,
Stories in tortillas told.
From jalapeños to corn delight,
I'm laughing hard, oh what a sight!

Chili peppers bring a burn,
Yet laughter's what I truly yearn.
With guacamole on my chin,
I savor every tasty win!

Layers and Laughter

Stack them high, tortillas meet,
Layers thick, such a treat!
A scoop of beans, a dollop of fun,
Who knew meals could be this pun?

Sour cream smiles, cheese so bright,
I'm dancing, what a sight!
Each layer speaks, each crunch resonates,
Laughter echoes, appetites inflate!

This dish a masterpiece on my plate,
A food fiesta to celebrate!
With friends beside, what could be better?
In taco joy, we write our letter!

A Symphony of Crunch and Cream

Harmonies of salsa collide,
With every bite, my taste buds ride.
Crispy edges, creamy flows,
A melody of flavors grows!

Each crunch delivers a little grin,
Who knew food could be such a win?
With every taco, laughter swells,
In this yummy universe, all is well!

Bite by bite, the laughter sings,
Wrapped in joy, oh how it clings.
Savor the moment, let worries cease,
In this fiesta, we find our peace!

Carried by Culinary Dreams

In a world of flavors wide,
Taco dreams are my guide.
Each filling tells a funny tale,
As I munch and laugh without fail!

From fish to beef, so much delight,
My taste buds dance with pure delight.
With every wrap, my heart takes flight,
In a taco haven, everything's right!

Savoring joy like it's a game,
Each taco twist, never the same.
With friends around, the table gleams,
We share our hopes and culinary dreams!

Life Between Two Tortillas

In a world wrapped tight, oh what a feast,
Crunchy corners crisp, where happiness creased.
Beans doing the cha-cha, rice in a spin,
With salsa so zesty, let the good times begin.

Avocado winks, and lime gives a zest,
Together we laugh, we savor the best.
From taco to taco, we'll travel this road,
Sharing each bite, lightening the load.

The Symphony of Spices

Under the sun, we dance and we jive,
While cumin and coriander vibe to survive.
Paprika's serenade, a twist in the air,
Laughter mingles here, flavors everywhere.

Tortillas flutter softly, like notes in the breeze,
A harmony rich, oh, won't you just please?
Each topping a solo, each crunch fills the night,
Together we feast, it's a pure delight.

A Bite of Joy

With a crunch and a munch, oh what a thrill,
Each bite like a hug; we savor and chill.
Cheese melting slowly, like moments divine,
Filling our hearts, one taco at a time.

The guac is a party, the chips join the show,
Sharing the flavor, letting joy overflow.
With every great laugh, and every good cheer,
We find our delight, it's all crystal clear.

Achieving Balance Through Flavor

In a world that keeps spinning, we find our way,
Balancing tastes in a bright gourmet play.
Some spice for the zest and some chill for the taste,
Life's better with tacos, let's not go to waste.

With layers of goodness, so rich and so bold,
Each bite is a story, each crunch to behold.
Finding that sweet spot, like salsa on chip,
With laughter and tacos, we sail on this trip.

A Journey of Spicy Layers

In a world where flavors dance,
I found a crunch, oh what a chance!
Lettuce whispers, cheese does tease,
In every bite, a taste of ease.

Tomatoes blush, jalapeños scream,
Salsa swirls, a vibrant dream.
Wrap it all in a warm embrace,
Adventure's waiting, let's make haste!

They say life's short, so bring the heat,
With every layer, a feast to eat.
A sprinkle of joy, a dash of fun,
Every taco makes the world more spun.

So grab a seat, let's share a laugh,
Under the stars, we'll write our path.
With guacamole smiles, cheers arise,
Taco tales beneath the skies.

The Perfect Blend of Ingredients

In a kitchen bright, where flavors mix,
A dash of laughter, some spicy tricks.
Beans and corn in a happy swirl,
Each bite a giggle, each taste a twirl.

Sizzle and pop, the pan's alive,
Ingredients dance, they love to thrive.
Crispy shells, golden and bold,
Wrapped in joy, stories unfold.

A sprinkle of love, a pinch of glee,
Making my meal a jubilee.
With every layer, a laugh to share,
In this feast, nothing's rare!

So raise a taco, let's toast the night,
Here's to the flavors that feel so right.
In the perfect blend, we all unite,
With smiles and bites, our hearts take flight.

Soft Corn Clouds and Chasing Rainbows

Soft corn clouds start to appear,
Beneath the sun, there's nothing to fear.
With every bite, we drift away,
To rainbow dreams where we can play.

Chasing flavors, wild and free,
A salsa waterfall, come dance with me!
In a world of zest, we laugh and sing,
Life's a taco—let the joy ring!

Crispy edges, a flavor burst,
In this taco land, we truly thirst.
Let's stack them high and share the fun,
With every crunch, our hearts are won.

So grab a friend, let's take a trip,
On this journey, we won't skip.
With soft corn clouds and laughter's glow,
Life is tasty, and love can grow!

Cilantro-Scented Delights

In a garden bright, the herbs do cheer,
Cilantro dances, the flavors are near.
With tiny bites, we're feeling grand,
Each taco's twist a taste so planned.

A sprinkle here and a zestful task,
What's in the wrap? Go on, just ask!
With every crunch, our spirits lift,
These taco tales, our greatest gift.

Laughing through bites, we sip our drinks,
Salsa dreams and happy winks.
With friends beside, the fun ignites,
In cilantro-scented, starry nights.

So let's embrace this taco spree,
Each flavor a line of poetry.
With laughter and joy, let's take a bite,
In this fiesta, everything feels right!

Toppings of Gratitude

Chili flakes and cheese on high,
Laughter served with a side of pie,
Guacamole's rich, so creamy and fine,
Each bite a joy, a taste divine.

Tortillas warm, wrapped in delight,
Joyful moments, a savory bite,
With every crunch, a smile does bloom,
Life's little blessings fill the room.

Step right up, I'll make you a feast,
A sprinkle of love, from the greatest to least,
Let's pile on toppings, make it a game,
In this taco world, we're all the same.

Cheers to the moments, all wrapped tight,
With a dash of lime, everything feels right,
So let's celebrate, in a scoop or a shell,
Gratitude flows, like stories to tell.

The Salsa Serenade

Dancing tomatoes, spicy and bold,
A melody of flavors, stories unfold,
Chop up the onions, add a twist and shout,
In every salsa jar, there's a party about.

Cilantro sways like a breeze in the air,
With lime's zing, joy's everywhere,
Each scoop a laugh, a song on the tongue,
In this vibrant feast, we all feel young.

Let's dip and dive, with tortilla chips,
As laughter flows, our sanity grips,
Each scoop's a memory, colorful and bright,
Join the salsa serenade, day or night.

Gather 'round, friends, it's a tasty affair,
In this tango of tastes, we're light as air,
With every bite, let your spirit soar,
In this salsa rhythm, who could ask for more?

Assembly of Flavors

At the table, a grand parade,
Beans and rice don't be afraid,
Pickled jalapeños, zest on the crown,
Building these tacos, let's not back down.

Each layer's a tale, a flavor so bright,
Wrapped up in goodness, pure delight,
A sprinkle of cheese, a dollop of cream,
In this assembly line, we're living the dream.

Let's pile it high, make it a mountain,
Laugh with each bite, let joy be the fountain,
Salsa flows freely, a cascade of cheer,
With friends by my side, there's nothing to fear.

So grab a shell, let's layer it right,
In this tasty venture, there's no end in sight,
Each flavor we stack brings us all near,
In this assembly of fun, we've got nothing to fear.

Tacos and Tender Memories

In the kitchen, aromas collide,
Where laughter and spices comfortably bide,
With each taco shared, a story unfurls,
Tender memories wrapped in corn swirls.

Filling with joy, what a delicious blend,
With friends and laughter, the fun won't end,
Sitting around, we savor and tease,
Creating a bond, that's sure to please.

With every bite, we reminisce,
About long-lost moments, a savory bliss,
Each taco tells tales of good times ahead,
In the warmth of our hearts, love is widespread.

So raise up your taco, let's cheer to the past,
For in these flavors, our joys are amassed,
With laughter as spice, our souls take flight,
In tacos and memories, everything feels right.

A Tasting of Time

In a world of shells and beef,
I found joy beyond belief.
Salsa drips like falling stars,
Every bite a laugh, not far.

Crunchy edges, flavors burst,
Riding waves of salsa's thirst.
Guacamole smiles in each scoop,
Life's a dance inside this loop.

Lettuce leaves like gentle breezes,
With each taco, joy increases.
Time's a feast, don't make it bland,
Hold a taco in your hand.

Celebrate with every taste,
In this moment, don't let it waste.
Every taco tells a tale,
Of journeys held in flavors pale.

Spice Trails of the Heart

In a buffet of dreams and schemes,
Tacos whisper silly memes.
Pulled pork and ribbons of cheese,
Love wrapped tight, it's sure to please.

Hot sauce laughs, a fiery kiss,
In every bite, there's boundless bliss.
Cilantro dances on the tongue,
With every laugh, our song is sung.

The taco truck is life on wheels,
Serving joy with spicy meals.
Throw in some lime, you'll see the spark,
In a bite, we leave the dark.

So gather 'round and share the fun,
Under the sky, we come undone.
With each taco shared, we're friends anew,
In each joyful bite, we've found our crew.

Chasing Happiness One Taco at a Time

When life hands me a heavy load,
I find my solace on this road.
Wrapped in tortillas, dreams take flight,
One bite in, everything feels right.

Soccer carts and late-night runs,
With salsa dreams and laughs like puns.
Filling bowls of chopped up cheer,
With each taste, worries disappear.

A dash of spice, a twist of lime,
In these moments, I find my rhyme.
So let's gather, enjoy the ride,
With tacos as our joyful guide.

In every crunch, a memory made,
Chasing happiness, never afraid.
One taco at a time, we say,
Let's laugh our cares and woes away.

Tasting the Essence of Life

In a world of spice and zest,
Filling dreams in every quest.
Laughter served on tortillas wide,
With salsa smiles, we take a ride.

Guacamole dreams in every bite,
Making Mondays feel just right.
Chips and dips, a joyful cheer,
Craving happiness, bring it here!

With every crunch, our worries fade,
In a taco truck, friendships made.
Lime it up, don't hold back!
In this feast, we lose the lack.

So grab a seat and join the fun,
Underneath the shining sun.
In layers of joy, we find our way,
Let the flavors brighten the day.

A Flavorful Odyssey

Beneath the stars, we gather round,
With laughter and spice, life's joys abound.
Stacks of tacos, piled high and bright,
A crunchy compass in the night.

Cilantro dreams in every fold,
Tales of salsa, spicy and bold.
Every bite a journey to explore,
In this kitchen, we find much more.

With lime so bright, and beans so sweet,
We dance to rhythms of every beat.
Fajitas flame and laughter flows,
In this odyssey, the joy just grows.

So raise a taco, toast the thrill,
Immersed in flavors, hearts to fill.
With every crunch, the night's alive,
In our taco tales, we truly thrive.

From Street Corn to Heart's Core

The street is alive with flavors strong,
Sweet corn dreams where we belong.
Tacos calling, a tasty lore,
With each bite, we want to explore.

Cheese that melts like silly smiles,
Filling hearts with joy for miles.
Hot sauce drips like summer rain,
In these moments, we lose the mundane.

With every crunch, we taste the sun,
Life's a feast that's not soon done.
Toppings piled, layers to savor,
In each morsel, we find our flavor.

So gather 'round with friends so dear,
With tacos close, we have no fear.
From street to heart, it's never a bore,
In bites of joy, we always want more.

Culinary Choreography

In the kitchen, we twist and turn,
With laughter and spice, our passions burn.
Slicing, dicing, a rolling dance,
Each taco made, a chance to prance.

Bowl of beans, a salsa thrill,
As we juggle flavors with skill.
Onions twirl and peppers sway,
In this choreography, we laugh and play.

Tortillas spinning, both soft and warm,
Creating magic, our perfect form.
With every wrap, a little cheer,
Our culinary dreams come alive here.

So let's dance to the rhythm of taste,
In this taco swirl, we'll never waste.
Life's too short for boring meals,
Join the fiesta, see how it feels!

The Crunch of Existence

In a world so filled with zest,
Crunchy shells put life to the test.
With every bite, a giggle flows,
Savoring laughter's tasty throes.

Lettuce leaves dance in the breeze,
Cheesy grins are sure to please.
Life's flavors mixed, a spicy blend,
In the kitchen, fun has no end.

A side of beans, a dollop of cream,
Life's riches wrapped, a tasty dream.
Chasing worries, let them run,
In each taco, there's silly fun!

So grab a seat, enjoy the feast,
Life's humor in a tortilla, at least.
With every crunch, the world turns bright,
Feeling merry by taco night!

Tortilla Dreams and Salsa Nights

Under stars with salsa flair,
Tortilla dreams hang in the air.
Guacamole smiles, a feast so wide,
Who knew chaos could be this fried?

Beans like magic, so full of cheer,
Wrapped in flavors we hold dear.
Jetting through spice on a flavor flight,
Each bite delivers a laugh, pure delight.

Dancing forks in a vibrant row,
Crunchy rhythms, the fun will flow.
In the kitchen, chaos can reign,
As long as tacos bring their gain!

So gather 'round for laughs and bites,
Life served best with funky sights.
Tortilla dreams on this wild ride,
In every taco, joy's our guide!

Wrapped in Flavorful Whimsy

A soft embrace in a crispy wrap,
Life's little quirks, a flavorful clap.
With a pinch of lime and a laugh so grand,
Taste buds frolic, at our command.

Chiles dancing with humor and flair,
Each ingredient whispers, "Do not despair!"
In the salsa's twirl, we find our tune,
Taco nights spark joy under the moon.

Folded laughter, spicy and fun,
Every taco's a chance to run.
Wrap it tight, let joy overflow,
In flavorful whimsy, our spirits grow!

So lift your forks, let's toast tonight,
Each bite a giggle, a pure delight.
Wrapped in joy, a banquet of cheer,
Savor the moments, year after year!

Happiness Served with Guacamole

With guacamole, life's a game,
A dollop of fun, never the same.
Tacos stacked high, a colorful sight,
In every layer, pure delight.

Cilantro confetti, so fresh and spry,
Each bite brings laughter, oh my, oh my!
Dancing between crunch and goo,
In a taco, we find the glue.

Sliced jalapeños, a spicy kiss,
Life bubbles over, a flavor bliss.
Crispy shells giggle under moonlight,
In every bite, there's woozy delight.

So gather your pals, let's make it right,
Happiness served on a taco night.
With laughter and guac, let joy reclaim,
In every mouthful, we're wild and untamed!

Palette of Moments

In a bustling kitchen, dreams collide,
Beans and salsa take us for a ride.
A sprinkle of zest, a dash of cheer,
With every bite, we gift a hearty jeer.

The crunch of lettuce, the melt of cheese,
Life's recipe stirs with such ease.
Laughter mixes with the seasoned air,
Each taco moment, we happily share.

When Ingredients Dance

Tortillas twirl like dancers in the night,
Filling up our spirits, what a sight!
Tomatoes tango, onions sway,
In this feast of joy, we laugh and play.

Guacamole joins, a creamy delight,
Together they groove, oh what a bite!
Salsas shimmy, spices ignite,
This playful medley makes everything right.

Filling the Plate of Existence

A plate before us, a canvas so bright,
Filled with treasures, a marvelous sight.
Cilantro whispers secrets so bold,
With every flavor, a story unfolds.

Crunch meets softness in perfect accord,
Like life's moments, we savor each word.
With blessing and taco, each second we cling,
In this banquet of laughter, we dance and we sing.

Threads of Flavor

With every layer, a thread is spun,
Beef and veggies unite, oh what fun!
A dollop of sour cream, a zing of lime,
We savor this tapestry, one tasty rhyme.

The joy of sharing with friends all around,
In this circle of flavor, true bliss is found.
Each bite a memory, a spark in our minds,
In the feast of our hearts, true happiness binds.

The Rumble of a Sizzling Pan

In the kitchen, things are hot,
The skillet sings, oh what a plot.
Sizzling dreams in a golden hue,
A dance of flavors, just for you.

Tortillas warm, a fragrant waft,
Crispy edges, a secret craft.
A splash of lime, a pinch of cheer,
Bite the bullet, the feast is near.

Beans and cheese in a lively fight,
Spices clash, oh what delight!
Chop it up, with laughter and zest,
In this chaotic, tasty quest.

So grab a plate, don't be so shy,
Let's fill it high and give a try.
With every crunch, joy is revealed,
In this wild world, supper's our shield.

Tales of Tasty Fortitude

Once I faced a mountain high,
A stack of nachos, oh my, oh my!
With every bite, the fortress swayed,
In cheesy glory, my fears delayed.

Salsa dripping like a tale,
A fiesta dance within a pail.
Each scoop a story, bold and grand,
In this crunchy world, we take a stand.

Guacamole, the smoothest of friends,
In dips and laughs, the fun never ends.
With friends around, we brave the plate,
Together we feast, and share our fate.

So raise a taco with smiles so bright,
With every flavor, we win the fight.
In tasty battles, we find our way,
Joy is served, hip-hip-hooray!

The Crunch That Heals

When life feels bland, and spirits sag,
A crispy shell is all I brag.
With every crunch, the world ignites,
A tasty remedy for tiny fights.

Fill it up with joy and spice,
A sprinkle of happiness feels so nice.
Each bite a hug, each flavor a cheer,
In every taco, love draws near.

Ranch and habanero swoosh and sway,
With every crunch, they brighten the day.
In this grand taco, my heart's revealed,
Healing laughter, in flavors concealed.

So join the feast, let's give a cheer,
For crunchy moments that draw us near.
With every bite, we mend and mend,
In this savory journey, we all transcend.

A Tasty Love Letter

Dear beloved, though we're far apart,
I send a wish from my crunchy heart.
Wrapped in warmth like a floury shell,
In every taco, I want to dwell.

Tomatoes glisten in the soft moonlight,
Like your smile, they make it right.
A dollop of sour cream, love's embrace,
In every bite, I find your grace.

You are the spice that makes me whole,
In this dinner dance, you play a role.
Through salsas sweet and flavors bold,
I write these words, a tale retold.

So take this meal, my heart's delight,
In every crunch, our worlds unite.
With taco dreams, our love I send,
Forever yours, my flavorful friend.

The Art of Folding Joy

In the kitchen, chaos reigns,
Flavors dance in joyful chains.
Chip and salsa, guac in sight,
A taco night feels just so right.

Rolling tortillas, the art we keep,
Filled with dreams that make us leap.
Cheese that melts and spices tease,
With every bite, we're sure to please.

Friends gather round, a joyous crowd,
Laughter echoes, isn't it loud?
Folding joy with every layer,
In this taco, we feel the player.

So let's celebrate, no time to fret,
With every crunch, we won't regret.
A silly feast on this fine night,
Under stars, everything feels right.

A Fiesta on My Plate

Colors burst, a visual feast,
A fiesta awaits, come join the beast.
Red and green, a salsa show,
This happy plate steals the show.

Toppings high, a glorious tower,
Chewy bites with spice and power.
Once shy veggies now come alive,
In this mix, they learn to thrive.

Wrap it up in crispy bliss,
Every mouthful feels like a kiss.
Friends and laughter fill the air,
Who knew joy could taste so rare?

With every crunch, the world feels bright,
As if we've shared a secret night.
A fiesta's born on our plates wide,
In taco magic, we take pride.

Whispers of Lime and Laughter

Zesty whispers linger near,
A sprinkle of lime, we cheer and peer.
In the clatter of plates, we find delight,
Taco tales under the moonlight.

With each squeeze, our worries dissolve,
In guacamole, we all evolve.
Sour or sweet, we taste the twist,
In every bite, joy can't be missed.

Gather 'round, the circle's tight,
Mix and mingle, oh what a sight!
Life's little quirks wrapped up in shells,
Sharing stories like ringing bells.

As laughter rolls like waves on sand,
Each taco crafted by loving hand.
In this fiesta, hearts will soar,
With whispers of lime, we crave for more.

Grains of Experience

Corn in my pocket, tales untold,
Life's a wrap, oh so bold.
With every grain, a lesson learned,
In the taco dreams, we've yearned.

Tortillas spin like stories shared,
Cradling moments, no one's spared.
Salsa drips with laughter's grace,
In this flavor, we find our place.

Every bite a memory made,
In the kitchen's warm charade.
From crunchy shells to soft delight,
Grains of experience feel so right.

So gather round, let's take a taste,
In cheesy joy, there's no time to waste.
Each taco tells a tale anew,
In grains of laughter, we break through.

Crunchy Echoes of Laughter

In a world of cheese and spice,
Every bite is pure delight.
Salsa dancing on my tongue,
With every crunch, my heart is young.

Beans and guac in a warm embrace,
Tortilla hugs, a savory chase.
Laughter rises like steam from meat,
Gather round, it's quite a treat!

Chasing flavors like a wild race,
Sour cream smiles on every face.
Each burrito's a joyful scream,
Life's a party, or so it seems.

So grab a fork, let's make a splash,
In this fiesta, we'll have a bash.
With crunchy echoes in the air,
Who needs regret? We just don't care!

A Roadside Feast of Gratitude

On this roadside, we feast with glee,
What's on the menu? Tacos, yippee!
Cilantro smiles, so fresh and bright,
Every bite is a pure delight.

Grilled tacos dance, a tasty tease,
Sweet corn whispers in the breeze.
With every crunch, my heart takes flight,
Feasting under the stars at night.

Lemon squeezes add some zing,
Each layer wraps joy, like a king.
In this moment, all worries fade,
With laughter shared, our joy is made.

So raise a taco and toast with cheer,
To roadside adventures with friends so dear.
Gratitude served on a tortilla plate,
Life's a feast, let's celebrate!

Melodies of Morsels

In kitchens bright, tunes do play,
Sizzling sounds guide the way.
Tacos twirl in a savory dance,
Each bite's a thrilling romance.

With every layer, a story unfolds,
Like notes in a song, each flavor bold.
Crispy shells sing under my bite,
A melody of joy feels so right.

Sour cream swirls like a gentle breeze,
As spices whizz, my mind's at ease.
Tacos are a symphony, don't you see?
Each morsel's harmony fills me with glee.

So grab a shell, let's join the fun,
In this feast, we're all one.
With melodies of morsels around,
We laugh and sing, joy abounds!

The Richness of Simplicity

Tortillas wrapped, love's pure embrace,
In simple bites, we find our place.
No need for gold, just salsa dreams,
In each layer, life brightly beams.

Beans and cheese, a match so fine,
With every taste, our hearts align.
Take a moment, feel the thrill,
In humble joy, we find our fill.

Crispy tacos, laughter flows,
In every crunch, our friendship grows.
No fancy meals, just share the plate,
In humble bites, we celebrate.

Let's savor life, let worries cease,
In every taco, we find our peace.
Richness blooms in what we see,
In simple joys, we truly be.

The Quest for the Perfect Bite.

In a search for a treasure, I roam the street,
Where savory tortillas and fillings meet.
With each tasty morsel, my heart takes flight,
Seeking the flavor that feels just right.

A dash of cilantro, a sprinkle of cheese,
The symphony of toppings aims to please.
With sauces so bold and spices so bright,
This culinary journey feels oh so right.

At times I stumble, and flavors clash,
Ordered a combo, but what a splash!
Yet I keep munching, through every bite,
Hoping the next one will be pure delight.

In dreams, I savor each hungry quest,
The perfect creation, where I'm feeling blessed.
Forks and fingers all ready for fights,
In the epic search for the best of bites.

Savory Whispers of Solace

In the quiet of lunch, I ponder my fate,
A tortilla wrapped tight, oh wouldn't it rate?
With beans so creamy and guac so divine,
A bite of pure comfort, like sipping on wine.

The crunch of the shell, it calls from afar,
My taco-filled heart is the real shining star.
With every fresh taco they serve with a grin,
I find my lost worries, and let the fun in.

Salsa in hand, I dance with delight,
Each fiery scoop puts my troubles to flight.
In laughter and spice, we'll sail through the day,
With tacos around us, who could feel gray?

With friends by my side, we savor each laugh,
As laughter and salsa become our true craft.
In this funny journey, our smiles take a chance,
For it's riskier not to—let's just taco dance!

In the Dance of Tortillas

Under the moon, tortillas twirl bright,
Filled up with goodness, they shine in the night.
A waltz of flavors, around I spin,
With each savory bite, the joy begins.

I gather my friends, we salsa and sway,
Chasing the food trucks that come out to play.
Cheesy enchiladas, with laughter they pair,
In the dance of tortillas, there's magic in the air.

The rhythmic crunch echoes under the stars,
As we feast on delights, forget our cars!
With jalapeños dancing, and laughter so bold,
Life's vibrant colors start to unfold.

In every warm bite, the night lifts us high,
Together we savor, as laughter draws nigh.
So hand me a taco, let's hit the sweet spot,
In the dance of tortillas, we'll savor a lot!

Salsa Dreams and Spicy Nights

Under the stars, my heart's in a whirl,
With salsa and spice, it's a flavor unfurl.
Fresh pico de gallo, all colors combine,
Each scoop tells a story, so divine.

I dream of the nights wrapped in tortilla hugs,
Where laughter flows easy, and life gives warmugs.
The crunch and the soft, a delightful embrace,
In this dance of salsa, we find our own space.

With a sprinkle of zest, we share in the fun,
As tacos unite us, our battles are won.
Around the campfire, we laugh and ignite,
With dreams of tomorrow spinning into the night.

So raise up your tacos, let's toast and delight,
For who needs a castle when there's tacos to bite?
In the glow of good friends, our spirits take flight,
In salsa dreams woven through spicy, sweet nights.

The Art of Filling Moments

In a shell of dreams, we pile and stack,
A dash of laughter, never looking back.
With spicy tales and silly cheese,
Life's simple joys aim to please.

A sprinkle of chaos, a droplet of zest,
In the dance of flavors, we are blessed.
From salsa to guac, each bite's a dive,
Let's roll with joy, and just feel alive.

When Ingredients Align

Lettuce whispers, 'Don't be shy!'
Tomatoes blushing as they comply.
A hint of lime joins in the fun,
Together they shine, a feast begun.

Tortillas twirl in a joyous spin,
As laughter rises, let the feast begin.
With every crunch, and every bite,
We toast to flavors that feel so right.

Love Wrapped in Corn

Corny moments wrapped up tight,
In every fold, there's pure delight.
With a dollop of love and a pinch of cheer,
Every bite shared, brings us near.

Jalapeños laugh, bringing heat to the show,
As we savor the warmth that love can bestow.
Together we munch, cheeky and bold,
In this wrap of happiness, stories unfold.

Fiesta Under the Stars

Beneath a sky of glittery lights,
Tacos are dancing through joyful nights.
With chips in hand and hearts so free,
We celebrate life's tasty jubilee.

Each bite a burst, a starry delight,
Seasoned friendships, so warm and bright.
In laughter, we gather, come one, come all,
Under the moon, we answer the call.